The
Ĥardy Fuchsia
Guide

Text and Photographs
By David Clark

Oakleigh Publications

Contents

Introduction

THE distinction between hardy and ordinary fuchsias cannot be defined precisely, as to some extent it depends on the area in which they are grown. In warm countries, where winter frost is uncommon, almost all fuchsias are hardy and they can be grown permanently out of doors with little or no protection. However, in very cold countries few plants will survive the winter without the help of a heated glasshouse. This book covers climatic areas between these two extremes and is devoted to plants that can be placed in the open garden and, apart from a top dressing of bracken or peat in the first winter, will survive considerable periods of cold weather without protection.

With a few exceptions, most fuchsias grown today are hybrids. These have been developed by many generations of cross fertilisation starting from species that were brought to Europe by early plant hunters. Fuchsia species are found in a number of countries, most commonly those in Central and South America. The climate in which they grow, varies for example, from tropical in Mexico to severe cold in Chile or Argentina. It follows that the best hardy fuchsias will have descended largely from crosses made between species found growing in cold countries or high areas in otherwise warm countries. Most of these species such as *F. magellanica* or *F. coccinea* have small flowers and it is for this reason that many of the most hardy fuchsias also have small flowers. Although certain cultivars (cultivated varieties) are inherently resistant to cold, other factors have to be considered. For example, some plants reliably survive cold weather but do not have the vigour to recover quickly enough, or flower early enough, to make an acceptable display the following summer.

It is the aim of many hybridisers to improve the range of hardy fuchsias by increasing the size of the blooms, particularly in the production of those with double flowers. Ultimately it is not always the largest or most colourful blooms that look best in the garden. Very often the most rewarding plants to grow are the early and free blooming single cultivars, regardless of flower size.

Introduction

Figure 1.

Parts of a Hardy Fuchsia.

Single flowered fuchsias have a corolla consisting of four petals. Semi-double flowers have five to eight petals and double flowers have more than eight petals. Species are, or once were, found growing naturally in the wild. Varieties are minor variations of species. Cultivars, (cultivated hybrids) are plants produced in cultivation mainly by a process of hybridising between the various species.

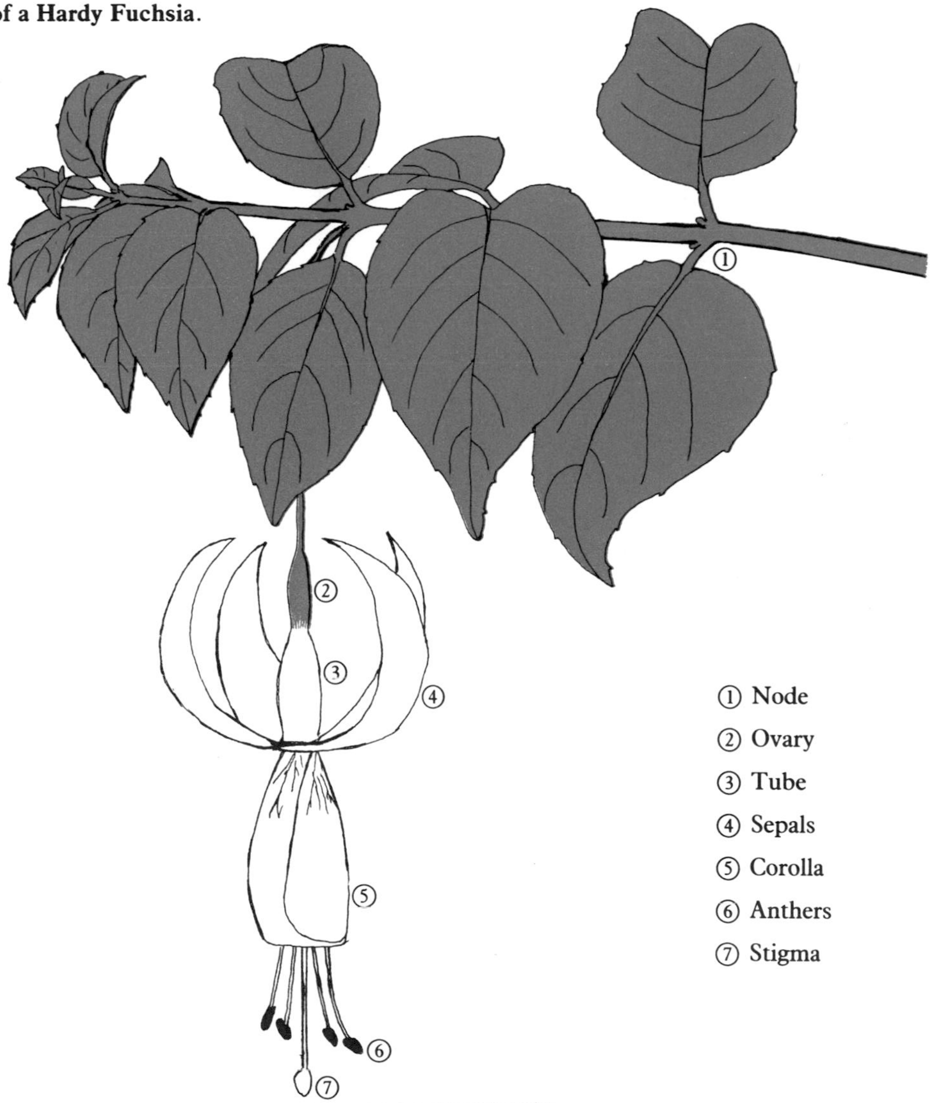

1. Node
2. Ovary
3. Tube
4. Sepals
5. Corolla
6. Anthers
7. Stigma

Cultivation of Hardy Fuchsias

FUCHSIAS are not demanding plants and they will grow in any normal well cultivated soil. However, they have a rather shallow root system and dislike long periods without rain. It follows that shallow soils, particularly if they are very open and do not retain moisture, are less suitable than soils with a high humus content. Fuchsias will grow in these areas providing they are well watered in dry weather and moisture conserving mulches of peat or garden compost are placed over the roots. Chalky soils are not inherently harmful but they are likely to dry out quickly and should be treated as described above.

As hardy fuchsias usually have a long life the soil should be well prepared before planting. The beds should be dug over in the autumn, and well rotted manure or garden compost worked-in to improve the soil structure and fertilise it. If these materials are not available peat can be used but as it does not contain any appreciable quantities of plant nutrients they should be applied in the form of a general fertiliser at planting time. Double digging is not normally necessary, for as mentioned above, fuchsias do not have a deeply penetrating root system. However if there is a hard crust or "pan" at about a spades depth this should be broken up and garden compost or peat worked into prevent it reforming.

Planting.

Small plants and rooted cuttings are not suitable for planting directly into open ground and should be grown on until they fill 10-13cm. (4-5in.) pots. Rooted cuttings, whether they are propagated by the grower or bought from a nursery, should be potted up in early spring into small containers no more than 8-9cm. (3-3½in.) in diameter. These small plants will probably have been rooted in a soil-less compost and it is good practise to continue their use at this stage. After potting the plants should be watered in and, if available, placed in a warm greenhouse to establish. After a few days it is essential to pinch out the growing tips to make them bushier. At this time the plants should be approximately 5-8cm. (2-3in.) tall and have 2-4 pairs of leaves. This is to ensure that when they are eventually planted in the garden, several stems will be buried below ground

Figure 2.

Planting Hardy Fuchsias.

Hardy fuchsias should be planted in a shallow depression in the ground. During the summer, this depression is gradually filled in. Before the onset of really cold weather, the ground should be level with the surrounding soil, and a 5-10cm (2-4in) layer of bracken or coarse peat spread around the plants, right up to the main stem.

level. This important factor can make all the difference to the plant surviving the first winter, as this time is the most critical period of its life. In three to five weeks the plants will be ready for potting-on into 10-13cm. (4-5in.) containers. On this occasion it is better to mix the soil-less potting compost with about 20% of coarse horticultural grit, ie. 1 part of grit to 4 parts of compost by volume. Sometimes the roots of plants growing in soil-less composts are reluctant to move from it into ordinary soil and the addition of a good quantity of coarse grit helps to alleviate the problem. Plants bought in large containers from the outside standing areas of garden centres should be ready for immediate planting.

The best time to plant hardy fuchsias is in spring after the danger of frost has past, but before the end of July. This gives them the maximum time to grow and establish before the onset of cold weather. Autumn planting is often recommended for other subjects but this is definitely not suitable for fuchsias. Greenhouse grown plants should first be hardened off by placing them out of doors for a few hours whenever the weather is warm, and then returning them to the greenhouse at night. This period of acclimatisation should be repeated whenever the conditions are favourable. The time left outside should also be increased gradually and after 10-20 days the plants should be ready for placing in the garden.

Planting should be carried out in the manner shown in figure 2. so that the soil level in the pot is about 10cm. (4in.) below the level of the surrounding soil. The covering of soil protects buds on the lower parts of the stems. In a severe winter, even if all the aerial parts are killed, the plant will still be able to send out new shoots from below ground. Finally work 60g (2oz.) of a general fertiliser such as "Growmore" into the surface soil around each plant and then water them in thoroughly using about 4.5 litres (1 gallon) per plant.

Treatment After Planting.

As soon as the new plants are in the open ground everything possible must be done to get them well established before winter. They should be generously watered whenever the soil around them dries. As mentioned above, fuchsias have a shallow root system and they can be severely checked, even by relatively short dry spells. Well established specimens, planted in earlier years, will also benefit greatly from additional watering during prolonged spells of drought.

Routine weeding and cultivation will gradually fill in the depression around the roots of the plants, but before the first frosts some extra coarse peat or bracken should be heaped over the soil up to the main stems. This extra protection should not be necessary in subsequent years.

Reasons For Failure During the First Winter.

In this section it is assumed that all the recommendations made earlier about planting, and treatment prior to the first winter, have been followed carefully.

A. Providing the cultivars being grown are genuinely hardy, losses due to cold should be minimal. However, locality and soil type play an important part and if plants only die in the most severe winters, replant with those given a higher hardiness rating in the chart on p. 27. As in most aspects of gardening there are anomalies to be found. For example 'Phyllis' is generally regarded as being a very hardy cultivar but it is unreliable in the author's own particular area. Similarly, many nurseries and garden centres sell 'Snowcap' as a hardy fuchsia but planting three well grown specimens every year for three seasons also resulted in a 100% loss. The reasons for individual failures are often obscure and difficult to explain.

B. It has been mentioned earlier that all aerial parts of stems can be killed in a severe winter and it is necessary for new shoots to be made from below ground level. Although they are not visible in an old and woody stem, the points from which the leaves once grew are the only places where new shoots can emerge. These potential points of growth could be as few as two depending on how much of the stem was buried below ground at planting time and the distance between nodes on the original cutting. The plant will fail in the spring if these tiny buds are eaten by insects, other animals, or killed by fungal diseases. If slugs and snails are a problem they can be deterred by using a proprietary bait or by spreading coarse sand or cinders around the stems at soil level.

The best way to avoid losses due to this cause is by planting bushy specimens so that the bases of several stems can be buried below soil level. Obviously the number of potential growth buds are multiplied by the number of stems, and therefore the chances of survival are much higher. Early pinching of young cuttings at the two to three leaf pair stage, will greatly improve the chances of their survival the following spring. The results of extensive trials has demonstrated that lack of growth points is the the most common reason for death of plants in their first year of life. After a few years the best hardy cultivars assure their permanence by the formation of a mass of stems originating from below ground level. This is the secret of their success and the reason why they are most vulnerable in the first winter.

C. Even if all of the above advice has been followed, a few plants of even the most hardy cultivars may still die. The reasons for this are obscure. Most gardeners have at some time prepared a bed with plants that look more or less identical, only to find that some thrive and others fail. This is a risk that all growers face and the only solution is to try again.

Pruning.

Under normal conditions hardy fuchsias need very little pruning and it is not absolutely necessary to prune them at all. In most circumstances do not attempt to prune until the end of May or June or whenever the plants start to make fresh growth. If all the new shoots come from low down on the stems, or from below ground level, it is probable that everything above that point has died. This can be confirmed by breaking off small pieces of the stems starting from the top. If the inside of the wood is green it is still alive, but a brown colour shows that it has died. If all the stems above ground have died, it is a good idea to prune away only half of their length. The remainder acts as a support and protection for the new stems as they grow, and will be quickly covered by the fresh foliage. After a mild winter, or if the plant is very hardy, it will start to grow from much higher up and become taller than the year before. Providing the plant has plenty of room to grow, this may be acceptable, but if space is limited it will do no harm to prune the plant back severely to limit its size. Healthy plants are seldom damaged, even by quite drastic surgery. Removal of small amounts of nuisance material growing over paths or in front of doorways, can be carried out safely at any time during the growing season.

Unless there is danger of autumn gales causing damage to the plants, they should not be pruned in the autumn or when dormant. It is only when growth starts in the spring that the extent of damage caused by cold weather can be seen. It is pointless to remove unnecessarily, potential areas of fresh growth. Hedges need dead, diseased, or nuisance material to be removed in the spring; no other pruning is necessary or required.

Feeding.

All plants should be fed in the spring when new growth starts to appear. It is a good time to feed all the plants immediately after any pruning has been carried out. "Growmore", or other general purpose fertiliser should then be worked into the surface of the soil around each of them. Small plants will need about 60g. (2oz.) and large plants up to 120g. (4oz.) each. Remember that fuchsias are shallow rooting and much of the root system will be close to the soil surface and easily damaged. John Innes base fertiliser can also be used for this purpose, as can any general purpose product containing approximately equal proportions of nitrogen, phoshorus and potassium. This balanced formulation will ensure that the plants grow away rapidly and replace growth lost in the winter. The speed with which this is carried out will, to a large extent, determine when the plant starts to flower. Time lost in the spring can delay the onset of blooming by several weeks. After the application of the fertiliser, and if rain is unlikely within 24 hours, the plants should be well watered-in.

Plants fed with a solid fertiliser, such as those recommended, will not need feeding again the same season. Later in the year it is essential that growth slows down naturally allowing the stems to harden and become more capable of withstanding cold weather.

Hedges.

Hedges are best planted in a shallow trench rather than the saucer shaped depressions described in figure 2. The planting distance depends on the cultivars or varieties chosen; some grow much wider than tall and the reverse is true with others. As a rough guide, plant at intervals between one and one half of the average height given in the chart on page 27. Fuchsia hedges should be regarded as a decorative feature rather than providing shelter to other plants. They should be situated where they are not exposed to strong, cold winds. The soil should be good and moisture retentive and the hedge should be in a position where it receives a reasonable amount of sunshine. Except for very mild areas only the most hardy cultivars are suitable and they should be chosen with reference to the chart mentioned above.

Always plant a hedge with one species or cultivar only as different plants growing in a mixed hedge never seem to harmonise. They tend to grow unevenly and create a ragged appearance that never looks tidy. The following is a list of fuchsias that are particularly recommended for planting as a hedge. Fuller details of each is given in the chapter starting on page 26, however, for convenience the approximate minimum heights are given here.

Cultivar, Species or Variety

Army Nurse 105cm (41in).
Blue Bush 100cm (39in).
Brilliant 70cm (28in).
Chillerton Beauty 65cm (26in).
Dorothy 72cm (30in).
Enfante Prodigue 90cm (35in).
Flash 90cm (35in).
Graf Witte 85cm (33in).
Madame Cornelissen 90cm (35in).

Cultivar, Species or Variety

magellanica v. macrostemma 'Versicolor'
                          120cm (48in)
magellanica v. gracilis 90cm (35in).
magellanica v. molinae 120cm (48in).
Margaret 120cm (48in).
Margaret Brown 100cm (39in).
Mrs Popple 120cm (48in).
Mrs W. P. Wood 120cm (48in).
Riccartonii 110cm (43in).
Whiteknights Pearl 100cm (39in).

Propagation

When hardy fuchsias are well established in the garden, they usually have a long and trouble free life. On occasions however, they grow too large or with hindsight it is realised that they have been planted in the wrong position. Sometimes plants have a sentimental value and must be left behind when moving house, or perhaps, new ones are needed to give to admiring friends or neighbours.

In all of these instances it is better to propagate new plants from cuttings. Although it is possible to move mature plants, it is usually quite hard work, and complete success cannot be guaranteed. Sometimes they will die and if only one plant is being grown the cultivar will be lost. Even at best, after moving a large plant it will take a season or two to fully recover. Therefore only a little time, if any, will be lost by starting again with new plants.

Propagation From Cuttings in the Spring.

In late spring, mature, well established plants usually produce a large number of new shoots. The tips of some of these non-flowering stems make ideal cuttings, and they will root quickly and easily without need for any special equipment such as a heated propagating frame. In the first spring after planting, fuchsias will probably have only a few shoots showing. It is then better to wait until autumn when they have had a chance to grow larger.

Only small pieces of the top of the stems are used, about 2.5-4.0cm. (1-1½in.) long. These should be carefully cut off using a very sharp knife or razor blade. Handle the cuttings gently to avoid bruising the soft young tissue and pull away carefully the lower leaves with a downwards motion: see figure 3 on the next page. The cuttings are then ready for insertion into the rooting medium. Unlike most other types of plant, it is not necessary to trim the cuttings to just below a node. At this time of year fuchsia cuttings root easily at any part of the stem. Hormone rooting compounds are not strictly necessary but those containing a fungicide will help to protect against rotting. However, this is unlikely unless contaminated or dirty materials are used.

Figure 3.

Preparation of Spring Cuttings.

Young cuttings are taken from the unflowering tips of new growth wh they emerge in late spring or early summer. They should root in abou 10 days at a temperature of 18⁰C. (65⁰F.). The cuttings need not be large, and ideally consist of a sturd shoot approximately 2.5cm (1in) i length, or even less, with two to th pairs of leaves. The cut can be ma anywhere on the stem and it is no necessary to trim to below a pair o leaves. Hormone rooting powders be used if desired, especially those contain a protective fungicide, but they are not strictly necessary with this type of cutting.

Cutting trimmed ready for planting.

Scale approximately 1½ times life size.

Figure 4.

Preparation of Autumn Cuttings.

is type of cutting is torn carefully
n the plant so it leaves a "heel" at
base of the stem. It should be
roximately 7.5-15cm (3-6in) in
gth and the lowest one or two
irs of leaves are removed before
ertion into the compost.
rmone rooting powders are helpful
t rooting might still be slow. If the
ting is taken rather late in the
son, the leaves may fall and the
ting not fully establish until the
owing spring.

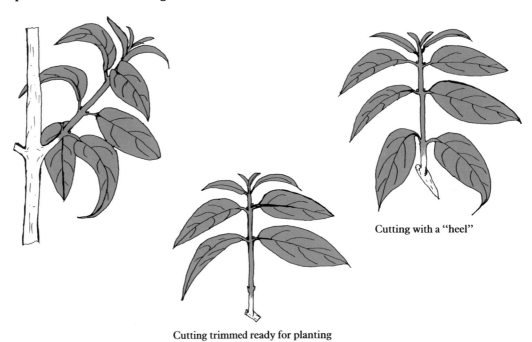

Cutting with a "heel"

Cutting trimmed ready for planting

Scale approximately life size.

Propagation From Cuttings in the Autumn

At this time of year, as soft unflowering tip cuttings are not available, it is necessary to modify the method of propagation outlined above and instead use larger, semi-hardwood stems. For this type of cutting choose small side branches between 8-15cm. (3-6in.) long. Preferably, these should still be growing at the tips, but just becoming woody where they join the main stem. Do not cut them off but rather tear them away so that they are still attached to a small piece of the main stem; see figure 4. The part of the main stem or "heel"

Figure 5.

Planting up Cuttings.

The diagrams show cuttings that ha[ve] been planted-up into various types [of] container. Always use a compost the[t] is suitable for seed sowing or rooting cuttings. If potting compost is used instead, the results will be unsatisfactory and many cuttings m[ay] fail to root.

Jiffy 7

Pot

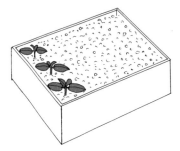

Tray

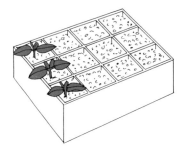

Individual partitioned container

as it is called, should be trimmed back slightly and the lower one to two pairs of leaves removed by pulling them off with a downwards motion. The cuttings can now be planted and housed, as described below, in a similar way to spring propagated cuttings. To get the best results at this time of year, hormone rooting preparations are very helpful, if not essential. The cuttings should be kept covered for a maximum of two weeks, after which, they can be gradually acclimatised to the open air before romoving the cover completely. Even at the optimum temperature of 18.5^0C. (65^0F.) the cuttings may take a long time to root. Some apparent failures may not establish themselves properly until the spring following a period of dormancy.

Planting Prepared Cuttings.

Plant up the cuttings in one of the ways shown in figure 5 and ensure that a seed sowing or cuttings compost is used. Potting compost is not suitable for propagation and will give noticeably inferior results. After planting, the cuttings should be well watered-in, preferably with a fungicidal solution to protect against the formation of botrytis. Fungicides containing the active ingredients 'benomyl', 'iprodione' or 'liquid copper' are suitable and should be made up at the strength recommended by the manufacturers for spraying.

If plant growth is suitable, cuttings can be taken in latc summer or early autumn, prepared as shown in figure 4, and planted directly around the mother plants in the open ground. It is unlikely that many of the newly rooted plants would survive the winter out of doors, so before the first frost, those that have rooted successfully should be carefully potted up and put in a heated greenhouse for the winter. The plants can then be placed in their final position the following spring after the danger of frost has passed.

After planting, the cuttings must be covered with a clear plastic film or similar light transmitting cover. This will help to keep a close and humid atmosphere around them until they have rooted. If cuttings are planted together in flower pots, each can be enclosed in a plastic bag, but larger quantities may need to be placed inside a small tent. A temporary shelter can easily be

Figure 6.

Protection of Cuttings During Propagation.

During the rooting process, it is vital that the cuttings are not allowed to wilt. To prevent this happening the are enclosed in a clear plastic bag or tent made from plastic film and wire or canes. Alternatively a heated propagating case is an ideal but more expensive solution.

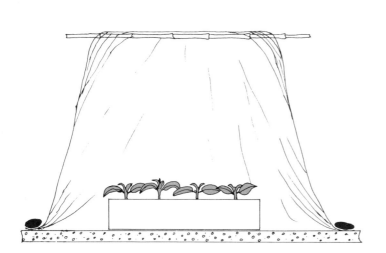

Cuttings under a protective tent

Cuttings covered with a plastic bag

constructed by using bamboo canes or wire covered with plastic sheeting; see figure 6. It is essential to provide a clear air space above the cuttings, and the leaves must not be allowed to touch the cover or they will remain wet and rot. A few loops of stiff wire inserted into the compost will prevent plastic bags from collapsing over cuttings planted in pots.

After planting, the cuttings should be placed in a greenhouse or on a windowsill. They must have a bright situation, but should not be in direct sunlight or they will shrivel and die. Sheets of newspaper, pinned up in strategic places in the greenhouse, will provide temporary shading while the cuttings are rooting. If a heated propagator is available that maintains a steady temperature of 18.5^{0}C. (65^{0}F.), the cuttings will start to root in 6-10 days. However, in an unheated greenhouse or in the home, the temperature is bound to fluctuate and rooting may take a little longer.

When cuttings begin to root, the leaves start to look brighter and appear more glossy. At this stage the plastic covering should be opened up slightly so that the young plants gradually become accustomed to the open air. It is important to remove the cover at the earliest possible time to prevent an attack by grey mould *(Botrytis cinerea.)*. Should this problem occur before the cuttings have rooted, pick off infected leaves and remove the cover as soon as possible.

Propagation From Seed

Seed can be bought from most leading seed merchants or it can be saved from the growers own plants. Germination of fuchsia seed is not high and a 30% success rate is quite normal. Most fuchsias are hybrids and crossing them often gives unpredictable results. Even though two very hardy cultivars are crossed, there can be no guarantee that the seedlings will have the same qualities as their parents. Unless the aim is to create new hardy hybrids, propagation from seed should be avoided. Many new introductions are the result of work by amateur growers and this aspect of growing can make a fascinating hobby. Unfortunately good plants are hard to produce and they should be tested for at least 3-4 years in a cold and exposed area before they can be regarded as potentially hardy.

Trials and Gardens

THE true merit of any hardy garden plant can only be found by extensive trials. Even if these are conscientiously carried out by the plant's raiser it is usually only conducted on one site. Obviously similar trials in other areas are required to ensure that the new cultivar is acceptably hardy throughout the country. Even with voluntary labour, coordinated trials conducted simultaneously at a number of sites are very expensive.

Many of the older fuchsias have been grown for a century or more and are cultivated in many different countries. By the knowledge that has accumulated over such a long period, those that are genuinely hardy have been identified by general consensus. Cultivars such as 'Charming' and 'Monsieur Thibaut' come into this category. Even so, opinions can vary and to avoid arguments, The British Fuchsia Society issues a list of cultivars that are accepted in hardy fuchsia competitions. This list is based mainly on accepted practise rather than on the results of trials.

To its credit, the Royal Horticultural Society has held a number of hardy fuchsia trials in its gardens at Wisley in Surrey. There were three trials conducted over the winters of 1963 and 1964, 1964 and 1965, and 1975 to 1977. A fairly good range of cultivars were submitted, ranging from those already accepted as hardy, to newer ones for an evaluation of their qualities. A list of those that gained an award are listed on page 29. The First Class Certificate is the highest award given, followed by the Award of Merit and Highly Commended Certificates. Although there are no trials currently being held at Wisley, a number of the cultivars that received the highest awards can be seen growing in the main garden areas.

The climatic conditions at Wisley are probably fairly typical of those found elsewhere in central Southern England and, as such, are not representative of many areas of Northern Britain or the rest of Europe. The British Fuchsia Society has a smaller more permanent trial being carried out at the Harlow Car Gardens near Harrogate and, close by, are beds planted by the Knaresborough Fuchsia Society. The climatic conditions of this trial are certainly more severe than at Wisley, but it is very likely that the cultivars and species that perform best are the same at both sites.

The author's trial ground is in Hampshire in Southern England. The site is open, very exposed, and at an altitude of 197m. (640ft.) above sea level. During severe storms in the winter of 1987 plants of 'Peggy King' were blown out of the ground and disappeared without trace. To date the majority of the plants have been grown for five winters and most of the details given in this book have been derived from the results of this trial.

Many gardens that are open to the public contain examples of hardy fuchsias, but apart from the trial grounds mentioned above at Wisley and Harlow Car, only small numbers are usually seen. Unlike roses for example, hardy fuchsias rarely have complete beds devoted to them. However, the following list of gardens usually have good displays during the late summer.

> Akenfield
> > at Charlsfield in Suffolk.
> Clapton Court Gardens
> > at Crewkerne in Somerset.
> Longleat House
> > at Longleat in Wiltshire.
> Powis Castle
> > at Welshpool in Powys.
> Wallington House
> > at Cambo in Northumberland.

Other exhibitions containing fuchsias can also be seen in public parks and at various flower shows held throughout the country. These displays will nearly always feature some pot grown specimens of hardy plants. The Chelsea Flower Show held in London and the Harrogate and Shrewsbury Flower Shows are always notable events and many leading growers exhibit there.

Pests, Diseases and Disorders

PESTS, diseases and disorders that attack fuchsias in the garden are not necessarily the same as those that cause problems in a conservatory or greenhouse. Under protection, the worst and most widespread pests are the glasshouse whitefly and western flower thrips. They are not usually a problem out of doors, but all the important pests, diseases and disorders are listed here because hardy fuchsias spend the first part of their life in a glasshouse, and are subject to the special problems involved there.

In the glasshouse it is vital to maintain cleanliness at all times, particularly by removing weeds and plant debris that can harbour pests. It is pointless to spend a great deal of time and money spraying plants if they are immediately reinfected from weeds growing under the staging.

Many growers do not like using chemicals, and biological control is a modern alternative. This method involves the introduction of an insect or plant that specifically parasitises the pest thereby reducing its population. Suppliers of these natural predators can be obtained by writing to the advice columns of gardening magazines enclosing a stamped addressed envelope for reply.

In the garden, the rosebay willow herb *(Epilobium angustifolium)* must be eliminated as it harbours the same rust disease that affects fuchsias. Most biological methods of control are not relevant to cultivation in the open garden, for without being enclosed in a confined space they are quickly dispersed. Luckily, plants growing permanently outdoors are usually much healthier and much less trouble than those cultivated in a glasshouse.

PESTS

Aphids (Greenfly) These are the familiar small green or blue insects that infest the growing tips of plants and can be troublesome both in the glasshouse and in the garden. Normally they should be controlled as they transmit virus diseases for which there is no cure. However, fuchsias are not normally troubled by viruses so unless the infestation is severe, treatment is optional. If control becomes necessary, most insecticides are effective against aphids, particularly those containing "pirimiphos methyl".

Caterpillars Normally the only caterpillars that attack fuchsias are those of the elephant hawk moth *(Deilephila elpenor)*. When fully grown, this caterpillar is 7.5cm. (3in.) long and can consume a great deal of the foliage. However, it is a very beautiful moth and not common, so it should be tolerated if at all possible. Hand removal of individual caterpillars is the best means of control.

Froghoppers (Cuckoo Spit) The nymphs (larvae) of these insects are found in the spring or early summer and are covered in a mass of frothy bubbles known as "cuckoo spit". They can cause considerable damage and should be controlled by washing away the bubbles with a jet of water before spraying them with an insecticide containing malathion.

Red Spider Mites The tiny mites are very small and virtually invisible to the naked eye. A severe infestation will cause the leaves to become yellow, mottled and fall prematurely. A fine web can often be seen on the undersides of the leaves. This is another pest that has become very resistant to insecticides, but spraying with malathion or diazinon can be tried. The mites are not true insects and chemicals that control them are correctly termed acaricides. This is a glasshouse pest and outdoor plants should not be affected. There are related mites that live in the garden but they do not seem to attack fuchsias.

Slugs and Snails These pests only seriously damage fuchsias in the late spring when new growth starts to emerge at ground level. If all the growing points are eaten away it can cause the death of the plant. Placing coarse cinders or similar gritty material around the base of the plants will deter these pests, or proprietary slug pellets or bait can be used to kill them. Always follow the precautionary instructions on the packet when using the latter method, or birds and other animals may be poisoned.

Beer traps are a safe alternative to using poisonous bait. They consist shallow containers filled with beer which are sunk into the ground up rim. The pests are attracted by the smell of the beer, fall in, and drown

Probably the most efficient and permanent way to control slu is to construct a wildlife pond. This need not be large and fish should be excluded. Very soon frogs and toads will breed there and effectively control their population and many other insects over a surprisingly wide area. Site the pond away from the house as the croaking of the frogs may cause sleepless nights!

Thrips The young are wingless and often less than 2mm. long. They lacerate the foliage near the top of stems and cause distortion of the growing tips. The winged adults are called thunderflies or thunderbugs. In recent years a new species of this pest known as western flower thrips has entered the UK on imported plants. It has swept through commercial glasshouses and at the present time 95% of all nurseries are infected. The pest is very difficult to control, even by commercial growers. The amateur can try spraying the plants with a 0.2% solution of sugar as this has been claimed to give reasonable control. Blue and yellow sticky traps can now be bought from large garden centres that attract and trap flying insects. The blue ones are said to be most efficient at catching this pest.

Outdoor plants should be sprayed once or twice with a systemic insecticide, but be sure to read the instructions on the bottle before purchase as fuchsias are damaged by some formulations.

Whiteflies (Glasshouse Whiteflies) These troublesome pests are like small white moths that make short flights when disturbed. They are now resistant to most chemical poisons and are very difficult to control. The young insects have a waxy coating to protect them and look like small scales adhering to the undersides of the leaves. The best control is obtained by spraying the plants forcibly, particularly to the undersides of the leaves, with a solution containing two to three drops of a good washing up liquid to each 600ml. (approximately 1 pint) of water. Alternatively, yellow sticky traps can be used to attract and trap flying insects. See also the section under the heading Thrips on this page. Although there is a species of whitefly that lives out of doors this rarely, if ever, fuchsias. This pest is the most troublesome nuisance to be experienced house growers.

DISEASES

Botrytis (Grey Mould) This aptly named fungal disease is encouraged by cool damp air and is usually encountered under glass in late autumn or early winter, but cuttings can also be affected during the rooting stages. The cure is to ventilate the glasshouse as much as possible and to spray the plants with a suspension of "benlate" fungicide. Pick off any badly infected leaves by hand and consign them to the wastebin.

Fuchsia Rust This is a very contagious fungal disease. It is characterised by pale yellow rounded spots on the uppersides of the leaves and raised gingery-brown circles on the corresponding part of the undersides of the leaves. Pick off any badly infected parts and spray with maneb, mancozeb, zineb or thiram sprays. The disease is also carried by rose bay willow herb and this weed should be eliminated from the garden.

DISORDERS

Bud Drop Sometimes flower buds are formed in the normal way but fall off the when they are partly grown. This is usually a symptom of dryness at the roots caused by dry weather. It can also be caused by root damage brought about by careless weeding at the base of the plants.

The former can be cured easily by copiously watering the plants and then spreading a moisture retaining mulch of peat or similar material around the roots. Continue to water the plants as long as the weather remains dry.

Poor Flowering This is very often caused by dryness at the roots and consequent bud drop. See the section above.

Rich soil or overfeeding will create lush growth at the expense of flowers. If this is the cause, little can be done immediately except to wait for nature to gradually deplete the soil. Otherwise root some cuttings and site them in a different position where the soil is normal. Some plants are more prone to producing excessive growth than others. *F. magellanica* and its varieties and hybrids are particularly susceptible.

Cultivars, Species and Varieties

THE main chart on pages 27-29 gives details of the height, hardiness rating and overall rating for the fuchsias depicted in colour on pages 33-48.

The **Heights** are the minimum that should be achieved 2-3 years after planting, assuming that the weather is severe enough to kill the aerial portions of the stems down to ground level each year. In mild areas, where fuchsias grow exceptionally well, such as parts of S.W. England, W. Scotland and Ireland, they will attain sizes much greater than those quoted.

The **Hardiness Rating** is shown by snowflake symbols which can be interpreted by the following table:

*	Hardy only in mild, sheltered areas.
**	Usually hardy except in the coldest areas.
***	Reliably hardy except in the very coldest areas.
****	Hardy almost anywhere.
*****	The most hardy rating; should be suitable almost anywhere that fuchsias are capable of being grown.

The **Overall Rating** is a personal assessment by the author based on the hardiness rating, earliness of flowering, duration of the flowering period, resistance of the blooms to weather damage, free flowering ability and appearance in the garden. Snowflake symbols are again used, five being the best rating.

Cultivars such as 'Snowcap' and 'Display' are often sold as hardy plants, but due to their poor performance in the trials they are not included in the charts.

The colour illustrations on pages 33-48 show flowers that are typical examples of each cultivar. The colours are as accurate as modern developments in printing and film technology allow. Depending on whether they are grown in a glasshouse or the garden, fuchsia flower colours can often vary.

Tables of Garden Performance
(For Those Cultivars Depicted in Colour on Pages 33-48)

Cultivar, Species or Variety	Height	Hardiness Rating	Overall Rating
Abbé Farges	45cm (18in)	***	***
Achievement	55cm (22in)	***	****
Alice Hoffman	35cm (14in)	***	***
Ariel	55cm (22in)	**	*
Army Nurse	105cm (41in)	****	****
Barbara	55cm (22in)	***	***
Beacon	60cm (24in)	****	****
Beacon Rosa	42cm (17in)	****	****
Belinda Allen	70cm (28in)	****	**
Blue Gown	70cm (28in)	****	****
Bouquet	30cm (12in)	***	***
Brilliant	70cm (28in)	****	****
Brutus	65cm (26in)	****	****
C. J. Howlett	50cm (20in)	***	***
Caledonia	65cm (26in)	****	***
Cardinal Farges	35cm (14in)	**	**
Carmen	45cm (18in)	****	****
Celia Smedley	76cm (30in)	*	**
Chance Encounter	45cm (18in)	*	**
Charming	80cm (31in)	****	****
Chillerton Beauty	65cm (26in)	****	***
Cliff's Hardy	55cm (22in)	**	*
Corallina	65cm (26in)	*****	***
Dollar Princess	40cm (16in)	****	****
Dorothea Flower	45cm (18in)	**	**
Elfin Glade	40cm (16in)	***	**
Enfante Prodigue	90cm (35in)	****	****
Eric's Hardy	45cm (18in)	*	**
Florence Turner	80cm (31in)	***	****
Garden News	60cm (24in)	****	*****
Glow	65cm (26in)	****	**
Gold Brocade	25cm (10in)	*	*
Golden Lena	35cm (14in)	*	**
Golondrina	50cm (20in)	****	**
Graf Witte	85cm (33in)	****	***
Greatham Mill	90cm (35in)	****	***
Gustave Doré	40cm (16in)	****	****

Cultivars, Species and Varieties

Cultivar, Species or Variety	Height	Hardiness Rating	Overall Rating
Happy	40cm (16in)	*	*
Heidi Ann	40cm (16in)	****	****
Herald	60cm (24in)	****	***
Howlett's Hardy	55cm (26in)	***	**
Jeane	70cm (28in)	****	*****
Lady Thumb	40cm (16in)	****	*****
Lena	50cm (20in)	****	***
Liebriez	25cm (10in)	***	***
Madame Cornelissen	90cm (35in)	****	***
magellanica gracilis	90cm (35in)	*****	***
magellanica molinae	120cm (48in)	*****	**
Margaret	120cm (48in)	****	****
Margaret Brown	100cm (39in)	****	****
Mary Thorne	40cm (16in)	**	***
Mauve Lace	70cm (28in)	**	***
microphylla	70cm (28in)	*	**
Mieke Meursing	35cm (14in)	**	***
Monsieur Thibaut	85cm (33in)	****	****
Mr A. Huggett	50cm (20in)	***	****
Mrs Popple	120cm (48in)	*****	*****
Nicola Jane	40cm (16in)	**	***
Papoose	30cm (12in)	****	***
Pee Wee Rose	70cm (28in)	***	***
Peggy King	75cm (30in)	***	***
Phyllis	70cm (28in)	*	***
Phyrne	65cm (26in)	***	**
Powder Puff	35cm (14in)	**	**
President	60cm (24in)	****	***
President Elliot	115cm (41in)	****	****
President Leo Boullemier	40cm (16in)	**	*
Preston Guild	50cm (20in)	***	****
procumbens	13cm (5in)	**	*
Prosperity	70cm (28in)	****	*****
Purple Splendour	55cm (22in)	***	****
Radcliffe Bedder	45cm (18in)	**	***
Radings Karin	45cm (18in)	*	*
Reading Show	55cm (22in)	***	***

Cultivars, Species and Varieties

Cultivar, Species or Variety	Height	Hardiness Rating	Overall Rating
Red Ace	65cm (26in)	***	***
Rose of Castile	45cm (18in)	**	***
Rose of Castile Improved	90cm (35in)	***	***
Rose Phenomenal	45cm (18in)	*	**
Royal Purple	45cm (18in)	**	**
Santa Cruz	60cm (24in)	***	***
Schneeball	65cm (26in)	***	***
Schneewitchen	45cm (18in)	**	***
Sealand Prince	90cm (35in)	****	***
Sharpitor	95cm (37in)	*****	***
Silverdale	55cm (22in)	***	**
Susan Travis	55cm (22in)	**	***
Tennessee Waltz	65cm (26in)	***	****
The Tarns	55cm (22in)	****	****
Thornley's Hardy	30cm (12in)	***	**
Tom Thumb	40cm (16in)	****	*****
Trase	45cm (18in)	****	****
Voltaire	65cm (26in)	**	***
Waldfee	110cm (43in)	****	**
White Pixie	55cm (22in)	****	***
Whiteknights Amethyst	100cm (39in)	****	*
Whiteknights Pearl	100cm (39in)	****	****

Fuchsias With The Royal Horticultural Society's Hardiness Award

FCC = First Class Certificate   **AM = Award of Merit**   **HC = Highly Commended**

Abbé Farges	HC	1965	Eva Boerg (= Lena)	AM	1962	Phenomenal	HC	1965
Abundance	AM	1978	Exoniensis	HC	1962	Phyrne	HC	1965
Bashful	AM	1978	Graf Witte	AM	1978	Pixie	HC	1978
Beacon	HC	1978	Isabel Ryan	HC	1978	Prelude (Blackwell)	AM	1962
Blue Bonnet	AM	1978	Lady Thumb	FCC	1978	President	HC	1965
Brilliant	AM	1962	Lena	AM	1978	Riccartonii	FCC	1978
Brutus	HC	1965	Madame Cornelissen	FCC	1978	Rufus	AM	1978
C. J. Howlett	AM	1978	*magellanica v. thompsonii*	AM	1965	Ruth	AM	1978
Chillerton Beauty	AM	1978	*magellanica v.*			Sealand Prince	AM	1965
Cliff's Hardy	AM	1978	*macro.*'Variegata'	HC	1962	Sharpitor	HC	1978
Corallina	HC	1962	Margaret	AM	1965	Susan Travis	HC	1978
Dollar Princess	HC	1965	Margaret Brown	HC	1965	Tennessee Waltz	HC	1965
Dorothy	HC	1965	Monsieur Thibaut	AM	1965	Tom Thumb	FCC	1962
Dr. Foster	AM	1965	Mrs Popple	FCC	1965	Trase	AM	1978
Enfante Prodigue	AM	1965	Pee Wee Rose	AM	1978	Trudy	HC	1978

Descriptions (Not Illustrated)

'BASHFUL'
Double or semi-double. The tube and sepals are a waxy red and the corolla is ivory white with red veining. The plant is dwarf, compact and very bushy. Although the flowers are small they are very freely produced. Very hardy and suitable for a rockery. It received the Royal Horticultural Society's Award of Merit in the 1975-1978 trials.
Raiser, Tabraham- 1974; Britain.
Height 55cm (22in).

'BLUE BONNET'
Double. The tube and sepals are red and the corolla is deep blue. The medium sized flowers are produced in great profusion and the growth is upright and bushy. Do not confuse this cultivar with the single flowered 'Blue Bonnet' raised in the same year by Hodges in the USA.
Raiser, Tabraham- 1950; Britain.
Height 45cm (18in).

'BLUE BUSH'
Single. This is an excellent, very hardy plant and is one of the best cultivars for planting as a hedge. The small to medium sized flowers have a deep pink tube and green tipped, pink sepals. The corolla is pale blue with a small pink basal patch with red veins. The growth is bushy, vigorous and upright.
Raiser, Gadsby- 1973; Britain.
Height 100cm. (39in).

'BORDER QUEEN'
Single. This cultivar needs a sheltered site but it is very attractive. The medium sized flowers have a pale pink tube and sepals and the corolla is violet flushed with pink. The growth is upright and free branching. It will not succeeed in all positions in the garden but is worth trying.
Raiser, Ryle-Atkinson- 1974; Britain.
Height 40cm (16in).

'CARNEA'
Single. This small, very bushy plant produces stems that grow horizontally. The small flowers are very freely produced and have a red tube and sepals and a deep bluish-purple corolla. This cultivar is sometimes sold as 'Peter Pan', which it does not resemble at all.
Raiser, Smith- 1861; Britain.
Height 50cm (20in).

'COACHMAN'
Single. No doubt many growers will never regard this fine cultivar as hardy; and they are probably right. It has medium sized tangerine orange flowers and unfortunately, there is no truly hardy plant with this colouration. However, 'Coachman' has survived three fairly mild winters in the author's trials. If an orange cultivar is required, this is the one to try, but for a very mild area only. Other near orange cultivars that have survived in the garden are 'Kolding Perle' and 'Lyes Unique'.
Raiser, Bright- ca.1910; Britain.
Height 35cm (14in).

'DOROTHY'
Single. The tube and sepals are deep red and the corolla is violet-blue veined with red. The medium sized flowers are very freely produced on an upright, bushy plant.
Raiser, Wood- 1946; Britain.
Height 72cm (30in).

'EMPRESS OF PRUSSIA'
Single. The medium sized flowers have a bright red tube and sepals and a reddish-magenta corolla with a paler basal patch. This is a very hardy and exceptionally free flowering cultivar. Unfortunately many nurseries supply 'Monsieur Thibaut' under this name.
Raiser, Hoppe- 1868; Britain.
Height 80cm (31in).

Cultivars, Species and Varieties

'EXONIENSIS'
Single. The rather long tube is deep crimson, the sepals are carmine, and the corolla is deep magenta. This is a very hardy plant but the freely produced flowers are small. The growth is weeping in habit and much wider than tall.
Raiser, Pince- 1842; Britain.
Height 30cm (24in).

'FLASH'
Single. The smallish flowers have a red tube and sepals and a magenta corolla that fades to red. The plant is hardy, upright in growth and reasonably bushy.
It is free flowering but not outstanding in this respect. 'Flash' was submitted for the Royal Horticultural Society's hardy fuchsia trial in 1975-1978 but was not given an award.
Raiser, Hazard & Hazard- about 1930; USA.
Height 90cm (35in).

'FRAU HILDE RADEMACHER'
Double. This is a beautiful cultivar very similar in appearance to 'Dark Eyes'. The medium-large sized flowers have a short red tube and red sepals and the full petalled corolla is deep blue. The growth is upright, bushy and has deep green leaves.
It needs a sheltered site to survive, but is worth trying as it is an exceptionally attractive cultivar.
Raiser, Rademacher- 1925; Germany.
Height 55cm (22in).

'GREY LADY'
Double. The tube and sepals are red and the corolla is a greyish-mauve. The medium sized flowers are freely produced on an upright, bushy plant.
Do not confuse this cultivar with 'Gray Lady' raised by Reiter in the USA.
Raiser, Tabraham- 1974; Britain.
Height 50cm (20in).

'ISABEL RYAN'
Single. The medium sized flowers are produced in great profusion on an upright, bushy plant. The tube and sepals are red and the corolla is white with noticeable pink veins.
Raiser, Tabraham- 1974; Britain.
Height 60cm (24in).

magellanica v. 'AUREA'
Single. The small, red and purple flowers are not produced in profusion but the deep golden-yellow foliage is the main attraction. The plant is very hardy and grows as an upright but slightly weeping bush.
Raiser, A variety of a species.
Height 60cm (24in).

'MAUVE WISP'
Double. The small flowers are produced in great profusion. The tube and sepals are red and the corolla is lavender-blue. This cultivar is fairly hardy and suitable for planting on rockeries.
Raiser, Tabraham- 1976; Britain.
Height 50cm (20in).

'MISSION BELLS'
Single. This is not usually regarded as being hardy but after one failure, three replacements fared well in the author's trials. The medium sized flowers have a red tube and sepals and a deepest indigo-blue corolla. The growth is upright but not particularly free branching.
Raiser, Walker & Jones- 1948; USA.
Height 55cm (22in).

'MRS W. P. WOOD'
Single. The flowers are very small but freely produced. The tube and sepals are pale pink and the corolla is white. This very hardy cultivar has light green leaves. It will make a good, but rather spreading hedge.
Raiser, Wood- 1949; Britain.
Height 120cm (48in) estimated.

Cultivars, Species and Varieties

'PIXIE'

Single. The deep pink tube is very short and bulbous and the reflexing sepals are also deep pink. The corolla is mauve but changes to pinkish mauve with age. The growth is strong and upright and the leaves are pale green, but darker than its sport 'White Pixie'. This cultivar should be hardy in all but the coldest areas.

Raiser, Russell- 1960; Britain.

Height 100cm (39in).

'PRELUDE'

Single. Do not confuse this plant with the double flowered cultivar with the same name raised in the USA by Kennett.

The medium sized flowers have a red tube and sepals and a magenta corolla. The flowers are freely produced on strong, upright stems.

Raiser, Blackwell- 1957; Britain.

Height 60cm (24in) estimated.

'QUEEN OF DERBY'

Double. The quite large flowers are very colourful. The tube and sepals are red and the corolla is blue with broad pink stripes. It looks very attractive in the garden but needs some shelter. The growth is upright but spreading.

Raiser, Gadsby- 1975; Britain.

Height 55cm (22in).

'RICCARTONII'

Single. The small to medium sized flowers have a red tube and sepals and purple corolla. This very hardy cultivar is frequently confused with varieties of *F. magellanica*. When fully mature, the sepals open flat and do not hang down. The growth is very strong and upright but rather open in habit.

Raiser, Young- 1830; Britain.

Height 110cm (43in).

'RUFUS'

Single. This cultivar is often erroneously called 'Rufus the Red'. The medium sized flowers are pure deep red and are freely produced on a strong but rather open plant. Although fairly hardy, it might need a sheltered position in the colder areas.

Raiser, Nelson- 1952; USA.

Height 50cm (20in) estimated.

'RUTH'

Single. The tube and sepals are deep pink and the corolla is magenta. The freely produced medium sized flowers are formed on an upright bushy plant.

Raiser, Wood- 1949; Britain.

Height 70cm (28in) estimated.

'TRUDY'

Single. This cultivar is rather similar in appearance to 'Chillerton Beauty'. The tube is greenish-pink and the upturned sepals are cream. The corolla is deep blue but ages to purple. The flowers are medium sized and produced on compact and bushy growth. It was not quite as hardy as 'Chillerton Beauty' in the author's trials.

Raiser, Gadsby- 1969; Britain.

Height 45cm (18in).

'WICKED QUEEN'

Double. The tube and sepals are red and the corolla is deep blue splashed with pink. The plant seems to be very hardy considering that the flowers are quite large. The plant is bushy and starts to flower fairly early in the garden. This cultivar is too new to be absolutely certain of its qualities, but so far it seems to be an excellent addition to the range.

Raiser, Tabraham- 1985; Britain.

Height 70 cm (28in).

'ABBÉ FARGES'

Semi-double. This cultivar is upright, bushy growth and the small flowers are very freely produced. The tube and recurved sepals are deep pink and the corolla is a greyish lilac-blue that changes to mauve with age. This cultivar received the R.H.S. Highly Commended Award in the 1965 trials.

Raiser, Lemoine- 1901; France.

'ARIEL'

Single. This is a member of the small flowered encliandra section. The tube and sepals are bright magenta and the corolla is pink. The growth is fairly strong and upright. The leaves are dark green and the flowers are followed by 8mm. diameter black berries.

Raiser, Travis- 1970; Britain.

'ACHIEVEMENT'

Single. This cultivar has a short red tube and fairly long red sepals. The corolla is purple and fades to reddish-purple. The growth is vigorous and in the form of a lax bush. The flowers are large with a corolla diameter of up to 28mm.

Raiser, Melville- 1886; Britain.

'ARMY NURSE'

Semi-double or double. The red tube is short and slightly bulbous. The red sepals only reflex slightly. The corolla is an unusual mauve-blue tinged with pink at the petal bases. The medium sized flowers are formed on upright, very vigorous bushy growth.

Raiser, Hodges- 1947; USA.

'ALICE HOFFMAN'

Double. The short tube and slightly recurving sepals are deep pink. The white corolla is flushed with pink and veined with red near the petal bases. Although the flowers are small they are freely produced. The growth is more broad than tall, bushy, and the leaves have a bronze tint.

Raiser, Klese- 1911; Germany.

'BARBARA'

Single. The short tube and sepals are pink and the corolla is a slightly deeper shade of pink. The freely produced medium sized flowers are formed on very strong, bushy, upright growth.

Raiser, Tolley- 1971; Britain.

'BEACON'
Single. The red tube is short and bulbous and the red sepals recurve slightly. The corolla is purple with red veining. The medium sized blooms are very freely produced on stiff upright stems.

Raiser, Bull- 1871; Britain.

'BLUE GOWN'
Double. For a large double this cultivar is free flowering and fairly vigorous in growth. The short tube and sepals are a shiny red and the beautifully formed corolla is deep blue with red splashes.

Raiser, Milne- date unknown; Britain.

'BEACON ROSA'
Single. This is a clear pink sport from 'Beacon' and the medium sized blooms are very freely produced. The growth is stiff, bushy and upright.

Raiser, Bûrgi-Ott- 1972; Switzerland.

'BOUQUET'
Semi-double or double. The flowers are small but very freely produced. The tube and sepals are light red and the corolla is deep indigo blue ageing to magenta. This is a fairly small, very bushy plant suitable for rockeries and is more upright and less spreading than 'Tom Thumb'.

Raiser, Lemoine- 1893; France.

'BELINDA ALLEN'
Single. The medium sized flowers have a long reddish tube and sepals. The corolla is pale blue. This strong growing and bushy cultivar flowers freely as a pot plant but is somewhat less floriferous in the garden.

Raiser, Gadsby- 1986; Britain.

'BRILLIANT'
Single or semi-double. The red tube is rather long and the red sepals recurve slightly. The medium sized flowers are freely produced on strong, rather open growth.

Raiser, Bull- 1865; Britain.

'BRUTUS'

Single. The medium sized flowers have a short red tube and slightly recurving red sepals. The corolla is deep purple with red veining at the base of the petals. The habit is vigorous, upright but somewhat spreading. This cultivar is excellent for most purposes and is very free flowering.

Raiser, Lemoine- 1897; France.

'CARDINAL FARGES'

Single or semi-double. The small to medium sized flowers have a shiny red tube and sepals and a white corolla with red veins. The growth is stiff and upright. This cultivar is a sport from 'Abbé Farges' but is less vigorous than its parent in the garden.

Raiser, Rawlins- 1958; Britain.

'C. J. HOWLETT'

Semi-double or double. The tube is red and the red sepals are green at the tips. The reddish-magenta corolla has two layers with a thin edging of orange around the petal edges. The flowers are medium sized and freely produced on stiff stems.

Raiser, Howlett- 1911; Britain.

'CARMEN'

Double. There are two cultivars with this name and they are frequently confused. The tube and recurving sepals are waxy red and the corolla is deep blue with red veining and pink at the petal bases. The medium sized flowers are very freely produced and the plant forms a dense low mound, much wider than it is tall. It is rather similar in appearance to 'Dollar Princess'.

Raiser, Lemoine- 1893; France.

'CALEDONIA'

Single. The red tube is long and the red sepals are narrow, curve downwards and do not open flat. The flowers are medium sized with a purplish-red corolla. The growth is moderately vigorous and upright but spreads more than the height.

Raiser, Lemoine- 1899; France.

'CELIA SMEDLEY'

Single. The tube and sepals are pink and the corolla is a delightful currant red. The medium sized flowers are freely produced on a vigorous, upright plant. It is only just hardy and needs a well sheltered position or mild site for it to succeed out of doors.

Raiser, Roe- 1970; Britain.

'CHANCE ENCOUNTER'
Single. This is another encliandra section member with tiny pink flowers and distinct white tips to the sepals. The leaves are very dark green and the flowers are followed by slightly oval black berries.

Raiser, Schneider- 1980; USA.

'CLIFF'S HARDY'
Single. The tube is pink an the sepals are pink with green tips. The corolla is mauve with a pale pink basal patch. The small flowers are produced on a very vigorous upright bush. In rich soils the plant can produce excessive growth at the expense of blooms. Good as a hedge.

Raiser, Gadsby- 1966; Britain.

'CHARMING'
Single. The long arching stems have slightly yellowish-green leaves. The medium sized red and purple flowers are very freely produced. This cultivar was given the R.H.S. Award of Merit in 1929.

Raiser, Lye- 1895; Britain.

'CORALLINA'
Single. This very vigorous cultivar grows very much wider than tall. The tube is red and the similarly coloured sepals hang downwards and do not recurve. The medium sized blooms come early and have a deep purple corolla and are produced on long arching stems. The leaves are dark green overlaid with red.

Raiser, Pince- 1844; Britain.

'CHILLERTON BEAUTY'
Single. The tube is pink on the side that faces the sun and cream on the shaded side. The pink sepals open flat, not usually recurving. The medium-small flowers have a blue corolla that fades to purplish-red. This cultivar is identical to 'Query'.

Raiser, Bass- 1847; Britain.

'DOLLAR PRINCESS'
Double. This is a superb, very bushy cultivar that forms a low mound, considerably wider than it is tall. The exquisitely formed medium sized flowers are similar to 'Carmen' and have a red tube and sepals with a deep blue-purple corolla. Also called 'Princess Dollar'.

Raiser, Lemoine- 1912 France.

'DOROTHEA FLOWER'
Single. This is not an exceptionally vigorous plant but has been reliably hardy in the author's trials. The small flowers are produced in great abundance. The tube and sepals are cream with a pink tinge and the corolla is pale mauve-blue changing to pinkish-mauve with age.

Raiser, Thornley- 1969; Britain.

'ERIC'S HARDY'
Semi-double. The tube and upturned sepals are pale pink and the corolla is deep blue but ages to mauve-red. The flowers are medium sized and very attractive but this cultivar needs a sheltered spot to survive.

Raiser, Weeks- 1986; Britain.

'ELFIN GLADE'
Single or semi-double. The bulbous tube is light red as are the green tipped sepals. The corolla is pale pink-mauve with red veins. The medium sized blooms are produced freely on stiff, rather upright growth.

Raiser, Colville- 1963; Britain.

'FLORENCE TURNER'
Single. The cream flushed, pink tube is very short and the sepals are cream with only a faint pink tinge. The corolla is mid pink with a near white patch at the base of each petal. This is an attractive and unusual cultivar and the medium sized flowers are freely produced on a vigorous, upright plant.

Raiser, Turner- 1955; Britain.

'ENFANTE PRODIGUE'
Double. This cultivar is also known as 'Prodigy'. The tube and sepals are deep red and the corolla is deep blue with a red patch at the base of each petal. The flowers are medium sized and very attractive. The growth is very vigorous and upright; about as broad as tall.

Raiser, Lemoine- 1887; France.

'GARDEN NEWS'
Double. This and 'Prosperity' are arguably the two best hardy double flowered cultivars available. 'Garden News' is reliably hardy and is always the first double to flower out of doors and beats 'Prosperity' by about five days. The short tube and sepals are pink and the corolla is magenta. The large flowers are freely produced until frost damages the plant in autumn.

Raiser, Handley- 1978; Britain.

'GLOW'
Single. The long tube and drooping sepals are red. The corolla is red with a wide purple edge but turns all red with age. The small flowers are freely produced but come rather late in the season. The growth is vigorous and upright with light green leaves.

Raiser, Wood- 1946; Britain.

'GOLONDRINA'
Single. The long tube and narrow sepals are red. The corolla is magenta with a paler patch at the base of the petals. The growth is bushy and vigorous and the leaves are pale green and rather pointed. The medium sized flowers appear rather late in the season.

Raiser, Niederholzer- 1941; USA.

'GOLD BROCADE'
Single. The foliage is the remarkable feature of this cultivar being golden-green heavily suffused with mahogany. The medium-large flowers have a red tube and sepals and a mauve corolla. The growth is bushy and self branching.

Raiser, Tabraham- 1976; Britain.

'GRAF WITTE'
Single. The small to medium sized flowers are freely produced on a vigorous upright bush. The foliage is yellowish-green. The tube and sepals are deep pink and the corolla deep blue with a pink basal patch and red veins.

Raiser, Lemoine- 1899; France.

'GOLDEN LENA'
Semi-double. This is a green and yellow foliaged sport of 'Lena' with slightly smaller but otherwise identical flowers. However its vigour is much less than its parent and it needs a sheltered spot with good soil to do really well. 'Golden Lena' is colourful even when out of flower.

Raiser, Nottingham- 1979; Britain.

'GREATHAM MILL'
Single. This is a little known cultivar raised in Hampshire. The plant is tall and not very free branching but very hardy. The medium-small flowers are red and mauve and produced very freely.

Raiser, Greatham Mill- date unknown; Britain.

'GUSTAVE DORÉ'
Double. The medium sized flowers have a deep pink tube and sepals and a creamy white corolla. The edges of the petals are broadly scalloped. This is an exceptionally free flowering plant and the growth is upright and very bushy.

Raiser, Lemoine- 1880; France.

'HERALD'
Single. The medium sized flowers are freely produced on an erect growing plant. The short tube and sepals are red and the corolla is bluish-purple with a pinkish-red patch at the base of the petals. The leaves are pale green.

Raiser, Lye- 1895; Britain.

'HAPPY'
Single. The plant has an upright rounded shape and is suitable for planting on rockeries. The small flowers have a light red bulbous tube and red sepals. The corolla is deep purplish-blue and ages to magenta. The plant is very free flowering and bushy.

Raiser, Tabraham- 1974; Britain.

'HOWLETT'S HARDY'
Single. The medium sized flowers have a red tube and sepals and a long deep blue corolla with a pinkish patch with red veins at the petal bases. The growth is moderately vigorous and the leaves are dark green.

Raiser, Howlett- 1952; Britain.

'HEIDI ANN'
Double. The leaves are dark green and the freely produced medium sized flowers have a red tube and sepals and a mauve corolla. The growth is very bushy and strong. 'Heidi Weiss' also called 'White Ann' is a sport from this cultivar that has a white corolla but it is not as vigorous as its progenitor.

Raiser, Smith- 1969; Britain.

'JEANE'
Single. This cultivar is usually met under the phonetically misspelt name of 'Genii'. The small red and purple flowers are produced in profusion on a very vigorous and densely bushy plant. The leaves are pale lemon yellow under glass and deep golden-yellow out of doors. The plant is very attractive even when out of flower.

Raiser, Reiter- 1951; USA.

'LADY THUMB'
Semi-double. The tube and sepals are deep pink and the corolla is creamy-white with red veins. The flowers are formed in profusion on a dense, bushy plant. This cultivar is a sport from 'Tom Thumb' and is equally hardy and like its progenitor, is an excellent subject for rockeries.

Raiser, Roe- 1966; Britain.

'MADAME CORNELISSEN'
Semi-double or double. The tube and recurving sepals are red and the corolla is milky white with red veins. The small flowers are very freely produced on strong upright growth. It received a First Class Certificate in the 1975-78 R.H.S. trials.

Raiser, Cornelissen- 1860; Belgium.

'LENA'
Single, semi-double or double. The tube and sepals are cream with a pale pink flush. The corolla is mauve-blue with pink splashes. The medium to large flowers are produced in profusion and only slightly later than 'Garden News' and 'Prosperity'. The garden performance of this cultivar is slightly spoilt by its rather sprawling growth. It is identical to 'Eva Boerg'.

Raiser, Bunney- 1862; Britain.

magellanica v. gracilis
Single. The tiny red and purple flowers are very freely produced. The growth is strong and the long, gracefully arching stems have bronze-green leaves.

Raiser, Variety of a species.

'LIEBRIEZ'
Semi-double. The short tube and sepals are pale red and the corolla is very pale pink veined with cerise. The rather lax growth is only moderately vigorous but the small-medium sized flowers are produced in great profusion.

Raiser, Kohene- 1874; Germany.

magellanica v. molinae
Single. The small flowers are rather variable in colour but are usually a very pale shade of lilac. The plant growth is strong, often too vigorous, and will grow to tree like proportions in a mild area. Sometimes called *magellanica v. alba*.

Raiser, Variety of a species.

'MARGARET'
...ouble or semi-double. The
...ry short tube is red and
...e similarly coloured sepals
...curve completely. The
...uish-purple corolla has red
...lashes and veins. The
...edium sized flowers are
...oduced on vigorous
...owth, approximately broad
... it is tall.

...aiser, Wood- about 1940;
...itain.

'MARGARET BROWN'
...ngle. The plant is very
...gorous and produces
...asses of small flowers of a
...arly one toned pink
...lour. The growth is very
...ushy, only slightly broader
...an tall.

...aiser, Wood- 1949; Britain.

'MARY THORNE'
...ngle. The short bulbous
...be and sepals are red. The
...rolla is deep magenta-
...urple and ages to magenta.
...e fairly large flowers are
...eely produced on a thick
...emmed upright plant. The
...rge, rounded, almost heart
...aped leaves are dark
...een.

...aiser, Thorne- 1954;
...itain.

'MAUVE LACE'
Double. The red tube is
short and slightly bulbous.
The red sepals are broad
and recurve. The deep
mauve-blue corolla is veined
with red and fades to
mauve. The growth is
moderately vigorous, fairly
bushy and the leaves have a
bronze tinge.

Raiser, Tabraham- 1974;
Britain.

microphylla
Single. This is a typical
member of the encliandra
section with a red tube and
sepals and pink corolla. The
small deep green leaves give
the plant a cool fern-like
appearance.

Raiser, A species from
Mexico.

'MIEKE MEURSING'
Semi-double. This cultivar
is also found under the
name 'Pink Spangles'. The
tube and sepals are red and
the corolla is pale pink with
red veining. The growth is
upright, compact and very
bushy and the flowers are
freely produced.

Raiser, Hopwood- 1968;
Britain.

'MONSIEUR THIBAUT'

Single. The bulbous tube and sepals are waxy red and the corolla is purple, virtually unchanging with age. The stems are very strong and upright and the leaves are dark green. The medium sized flowers are produced freely and early. This cultivar seems to be confused with several others and many nurseries supply it as 'Empress of Prussia' or 'Phoenix'.

Raiser, Lemoine- 1898; France.

'NICOLA JANE'

Double. This is a nice medium to large flowered cultivar with a deep pink tube and sepals and a mauve-pink corolla veined with red. The plant is bus and very free flowering.

Raiser, Dawson- 1959; Britain.

'MR A. HUGGETT'

Single. The red tube is short and the red sepals are spreading but do not recurve. The corolla is mauve but with a pronounced paler edge to the petals. The small flowers are very freely produced on a compact, bushy plant. It is excellent in the garden and as a pot plant.

Raiser, Origin unknown.

'PAPOOSE'

Semi-double. The small flowers are produced in great profusion on a dense bushy plant that forms a l flattened mound very muc wider than tall. The tube and sepals are red and the corolla is very dark purple

Raiser, Reedstrom- 1960; USA.

'MRS POPPLE'

Single. This is one of the best and most hardy fuchsias and makes an excellent hedge. The medium sized flowers are red and purple and the leaves are a very deep green. It is always among the first of the hardy fuchsias to flower in the garden and one of the last to stop flowering in autumn. It received the R.H.S. First Class Certificate in the 1963 trials.

Raiser, Elliott- 1899; Britain.

'PEE WEE ROSE'

Single or semi-double. Th medium to small flowers have a fairly long red tube and short red sepals. The corolla is mauve-red but fades to red. The growth i vigorous but only moderately bushy. This cultivar received the R.H.S Award of Merit in the 197 trials.

Raiser, Niederholzer- 1939 USA.

'EGGY KING'

ingle. The short tube and ightly recurved sepals are axy red. The corolla is ddish-purple and fades to lighter shade of the same lour. The growth is right and very vigorous t not very free branching, rticularly near ground vel.

aiser, Wood- 1954; Britain.

'POWDER PUFF'

Double. Do not confuse this cultivar with a non-hardy plant bearing the same name raised in the USA by Hodges. The short tube and sepals are deep pink and the milky white corolla is lightly veined with red. The small blooms are produced in profusion and the growth is very bushy.

Raiser, Tabraham- 1976; Britain.

'HYLLIS'

emi-double. This cultivar generally regarded as ing very hardy but 3 out 4 plants died in the first inter of the author's trials. he broad tube and sepals re waxy red and the corolla red, almost magenta. The edium sized flowers re freely produced on an pright, fairly bushy plant.

aiser, Brown- 1938; ritain.

'PRESIDENT'

Semi-double or single. The bulbous tube and sepals are red and the corolla is purplish-red fading to red. The medium sized flowers are produced on long arching stems and the plant is only moderately bushy. The leaves are large and dark green with a pronounced bronze tint.

Raiser, Standish- 1841; Britain.

'HYRNE'

ouble. This is an nteresting plant with large owers. The tube and sepals re red and the corolla is ilky white, heavily veined nd splashed with red. The ather crinkled leaves are ark green and the stems re red.

aiser, Lemoine- 1905; rance.

'PRESIDENT ELLIOT'

Single. The medium sized flowers have a long bulbous red tube and red sepals. The corolla is reddish-purple. The growth is extremely strong, upright and fairly bushy.

Raiser, Thorne- 1962; Britain.

'PRESIDENT LEO BOULLEMIER'
Single. The plant is exceptionally bushy and free branching. The medium sized flowers are freely produced but unfortunately rather late in the season. The tube and sepals are virtually white and the corolla is deep blue.

Raiser, Burns- 1983; Britain.

'PROSPERITY'
Double. The large flowers are freely produced on very strong upright stems. This cultivar blooms very early the garden and only a few days after 'Garden News'. The tube and sepals are re and the corolla is pale pink heavily veined with red an flushed with red at the bas of the petals.

Raiser, Gadsby- 1979; Britain.

'PRESTON GUILD'
Single. The flowers are small to medium sized but very freely produced on vigorous upright stems. The tube and sepals are white and the corolla is sky blue but fades to almost red giving the plant the appearance of having two completely different coloured flowers.

Raiser, Thornley- 1971; Britain.

'PURPLE SPLENDOUR'
Double. The bulbous tube and slightly recurving sepa are red. The corolla is tightly packed with deep blue petals that fade to purple with age. The flowe are large and the growth is upright and bushy but rather spreading. This cultivar received the R.H.S Highly Commended Certificate in the 1975 trial

Raiser, Sunningdale Nurseries- 1975; Britain.

procumbens
Single. This unusual species has long trailing stems that creep over the ground. The small flowers have a yellow tube and dark purple and green sepals. The pollen is bright blue. The flowers are followed by large plum coloured fruits. The small heart shaped leaves are produced on thin, wiry stems. This cultivar is very hardy providing drainage is good, eg as a rockery plant.

Raiser, A species from New Zealand.

'RADCLIFFE BEDDER'
Single or semi-double. Thi cultivar has tall, upright growth and is very free flowering. The medium sized blooms have a short red tube and red sepals tha recurve to touch the tube. The corolla is bluish-purpl with a pink basal patch an red veins.

Raiser, Roe- 1980; Britain.

'ADINGS KARIN'
ngle. This is an encliandra
e with tiny leaves and
wers. The tube and sepals
light magenta-red and
corolla is orange-red.
e flowers are followed by
nd, black, bead like
its. The growth is
orous and spreading but
ly moderately bushy.

iser, Reimann- ca.1983;
e Netherlands.

'ROSE OF CASTILE'
Single. The tube and sepals
are white and the corolla is
light purple. The flowers are
small but this is one of the
most free flowering of all
fuchsias and needs a
sheltered position in the
garden.

Raiser, Banks- 1855;
Britain.

'EADING SHOW'
ouble. The short tube and
pals are red. The corolla is
ep blue with a reddish
al patch. The medium
ed flowers are freely
oduced on upright bushy
owth.

iser, Wilson- 1967;
ritain.

**'ROSE OF CASTILE
IMPROVED'**
Single. The slightly bulbous
tube is greenish-cream and
the sepals are cream with a
pink tinge on the upper
surface and pink
underneath. The long
corolla is plum purple. The
medium sized flowers are
freely produced on a
vigorous upright plant. This
cultivar is superior to 'Rose
of Castile' in the garden but
inferior as a pot plant.

Raiser, Banks- 1869;
Britain.

'RED ACE'
ouble. The medium sized
owers are a more or less
e toned dusky red. The
owers are produced on a
ry strong bushy plant with
ightly yellowish-green
aves. Tested for four years
s hardy in the author's
ials.

aiser, Roe- 1983; Britain.

'ROSE PHENOMENAL'
Double. The large flowers
are produced on an upright,
reasonably bushy plant. The
tube and sepals are red and
the full petalled corolla is a
mauve-pink colour. It is a
sport from 'Phenomenal' but
unfortunately not as hardy
as its parent.

Raiser, Uncertain.

'ROYAL PURPLE'

Semi-double. The short tube and slightly recurved sepals are red and the corolla is purple with a reddish basal patch and red veins. The medium sized flowers are very freely produced. Many nurseries supply this cultivar as 'Dr Foster', which is similar but lacks the paler basal patch.

Raiser, Lemoine- 1896; France.

'SCHNEEWITCHEN'

Single. This is another cultivar with doubtful origins and along with oth cultivars it is also sold as 'Schneewitcher'. The shor tube is red and the similar coloured sepals have green tips. The flaring corolla is deep blue with a pink basa patch. The medium-large flowers are exceptionally freely produced on stiff upright stems.

Raiser, Klein- 1878; Germany.

'SANTA CRUZ'

Double or semi-double. The tube is bright red and the red sepals recurve to touch the tube. The corolla is purplish-red and fades with age to pure deep red. The medium to large flowers are formed on a strong upright growing plant but it is not particularly bushy.

Raiser, Tiret- 1947; USA.

'SEALAND PRINCE'

Single. The short tube and narrow twisted sepals are pink. The mid blue corolla has a red veined pink patch at the base of the petals. The medium sized flowers are produced on a strong, upright growing plant with light green leaves. It received the R.H.S. Award of Merit in the 1975 trials.

Raiser, Walker- 1967; Britain.

'SCHNEEBALL'

Double. The illustration shows the plant in general cultivation under this name in England but it is unlikely that this is the cultivar raised by Twrdy in Germany. The flowers are large with a red tube and sepals and white corolla. The flowers are freely produced on moderately vigorous, upright stems.

Raiser, Uncertain.

'SHARPITOR'

Single. This is an attractive plant with sage green and yellow leaves. The small flowers are pale pink but in the author's trials, were no very freely produced. The growth is strong and rather spreading. 'Sharpitor' is a variegated leaf sport from *F magellanica v. molinae.* It received the R.H.S. Highly Commended Award in the 1975 trials.

Raiser, National Trust- ca.1974; Britain.

'VERDALE'
...le. This plant is like a
...der and less vigorous
...on of *F. magellanica v.*
...ae. In all but the most
...e conditions this can be
...dvantage but
...rtunately it is only
...erately free flowering.

...er, Travis- 1962;
...ain.

'THE TARNS'
Single. The short tube and
slightly recurving sepals are
pink. The mid blue corolla
has a white or pale pink
patch at the base of the
petals. The freely produced
flowers are medium sized
and the plant is bushy and
upright.

Raiser, Travis- 1962;
Britain.

...SAN TRAVIS'
...le. The rather long
...ous tube is pink. The
...ls are pink shading to
...m with green at the tips
...the corolla is
...vish-pink. The medium
... flowers are freely
...uced and the leaves are
...ish-green.

...er, Travis- 1958;
...ain.

'THORNLEY'S HARDY'
Single. This cultivar is
exceptionally free flowering
but the very lax, sprawling
habit reduces its usefulness
as a garden plant. The
flowers are small and have a
greenish-cream tube and
sepals and a deep rose-pink
corolla.

Raiser, Thornley- 1970;
Britain.

...NNESSEE WALTZ'
...ble. The flowers are
...e and freely produced on
...shy upright plant. The
...e and sepals are deep
...k and the corolla is
...ish-mauve splashed with
...k. It received the R.H.S.
...hly Commended
...tificate in the 1963 trials.

...ser, Walker and Jones-
...; USA.

'TOM THUMB'
Single or semi-double. The
tube and sepals are red and
the corolla is purple. The
flowers are very freely
produced on a compact very
bushy plant. This superb
cultivar, like its sports
'Lady Thumb' and 'Son of
Thumb', makes an excellent
subject for a rockery. It
received the R.H.S. First
Class Certificate in the 1962
trials.

Raiser, Baudinat- 1850;
France.

'TRASE'
Double. The tube and non reflexing sepals are red. The corolla is pale pink and flushed and veined with deeper pink. It is fairly vigorous and upright and the medium sized flowers are very freely produced. It received the R.H.S. Award of Merit in the 1975 trials.

Raiser, Dawson- 1959; Britain.

'WHITE PIXIE'
Single. This is a sport from 'Pixie' which is itself a sport from 'Graf Witte'. The very short tube and sepals are red and the corolla is milky white veined with red. The growth is upright and vigorous and the leaves are yellowish-green. The flowers are small but they are freely produced and show up well in the garden.

Raiser, Merrist Wood- 1966 Britain.

'VOLTAIRE'
Single. The bulbous tube and sepals are deep pink and the corolla is pale magenta with red veining. The plant forms a very vigorous upright bush and is very free flowering. The medium sized blooms are produced early in the season.

Raiser, Lemoine- 1897; France.

'WHITEKNIGHTS AMETHYST'
Single. The small flowers have a dullish magenta tube and sepals. The corolla is very deep purple, almost black. The plant is very tall, vigorous and bushy but in the author's trials not very free flowering. The plant is very hardy but is interesting rather than decorative.

Raiser, Wright- 1977; Britain.

'WALDFEE'
Single. This is an encliandra section member with very small scarlet and mauve flowers. The small leaves are formed on strong upright stems.

Raiser, Travis- 1973; Britain.

'WHITEKNIGHTS PEARL'
Single. The long tube and sepals are cream or faintly tinged with pink. The corolla is a nice clear pink colour. The small-medium sized flowers are produced on very vigorous growth with light green stems and slightly saw edged leaves. The habit is upright and bushy.

Raiser, Wright- 1980; Britain.